Confronting Jesus
Study Guide

9 Encounters with the Hero of the Gospels

Rebecca McLaughlin

:: CROSSWAY®

WHEATON, ILLINOIS

Confronting Jesus Study Guide: 9 Encounters with the Hero of the Gospels
Copyright © 2022 by Rebecca McLaughlin
Published by Crossway
       1300 Crescent Street
       Wheaton, Illinois 60187

Cover design: Josh Dennis, Jordan Singer

First printing 2022

Printed in the United States of America

Scripture quotations are from the ESV® Bible (The Holy Bible, English Standard Version®), copyright © 2001 by Crossway, a publishing ministry of Good News Publishers. Used by permission. All rights reserved. The ESV text may not be quoted in any publication made available to the public by a Creative Commons license. The ESV may not be translated into any other language.

All emphases in Scripture quotations have been added by the author.

Trade paperback ISBN: 978-1-4335-8301-8
ePub ISBN: 978-1-4335-8304-9
PDF ISBN: 978-1-4335-8302-5
Mobipocket ISBN: 978-1-4335-8303-2

Crossway is a publishing ministry of Good News Publishers.

LB		31	30	29	28	27	26	25	24	23	22
15	14	13	12	11	10	9	8	7	6	5	4	3	2	1

Contents

Preface

I'M SO GLAD YOU'VE CHOSEN to spend your time studying *Confronting Jesus*! I don't know if you're completely new to reading the Bible, or if you've read it all your life. I don't know if you'd call yourself a follower of Jesus, or if you aren't sure that Jesus even existed in history. I don't know if you're jazzed to read this book, or if you're reading it to please someone else. So I've tried to write discussion questions that will allow people with diverse backgrounds, perspectives, and experiences to talk meaningfully together about Jesus.

If you're not sure what you think of Jesus, or if you're pretty sure he's not everything Christians claim he is, please feel free to bring your hardest questions to the group. Don't worry about offending people. Your questions about Jesus are too important to keep quiet or to hold back. You might also be interested in taking a look at my first book, *Confronting Christianity: 12 Hard Questions for the World's Largest Religion* (Crossway, 2019), where I try to address tough questions like, "Hasn't science disproved Christianity?," "Isn't Christianity homophobic?," and "How could a loving God allow so much suffering?"

If you're a follower of Jesus already and you're reading with Christian friends, I hope you'll find the questions useful too. If you find the book helpful, maybe you can work through it again with a friend who isn't yet sure what to think about Jesus.

Whoever you are, thank you for taking time to read this book! I learned a lot about Jesus from writing it. I'm praying that you'll learn more about Jesus from reading it. But it's a dangerous prayer, because when we truly meet with Jesus, he changes everything.

Introduction

1. If you were to give your own one-sentence description of who you think Jesus is, what would it be?

_____

_____

_____

_____

_____

2. How would you describe your own spiritual background and beliefs?

_____

_____

_____

_____

_____

3. Do you think of the Gospel accounts of Jesus's life (Matthew, Mark, Luke, and John) being more like musicals, trying to capture the spirit of the hero—or more like biographies, trying to give a faithful account of the main events in a person's life? Why?

4. As you begin reading *Confronting Jesus*, which word most describes you and why?

   a. Curious

   b. Skeptical

   c. Eager

   d. Unsure

   e. Other (please specify!)

5. What are the biggest questions you hope this book will help you answer?

_____

_____

_____

_____

_____

_____

1

Jesus the Jew

1. To what extent have you thought about Jesus being Jewish? What difference do you think Jesus's Jewish identity makes to how we think about him and about Christianity today?

_____

_____

_____

_____

_____

_____

2. What parts of the story of the Jewish people before Jesus's birth did you find most interesting and why? (pp. 20–27)

_____

_____

_____

3. To what extent have you thought about Jesus being a member of a subjugated ethnic group, thousands of whom were crucified by the Romans in the region where he grew up? (pp. 27–28)

4. Have you ever asked yourself (or been asked) the question, how do we know that Jesus even existed? How would you answer that question after reading pages 28–29?

5. The first Gospel (Mark) was likely written down thirty-five to forty-five years after Jesus's death. If you're old enough to remember things that happened that long ago, what memories stand out most? If you're not old enough, what story have you been told by a parent or grandparent from about that long ago that's impacted you?

_____

_____

_____

_____

_____

6. Do you think it's plausible to believe that a person could remember something that happened decades ago if that event changed the course of his life, like Bryan Stevenson's visit to death row? (pp. 30–32)

_____

_____

_____

_____

_____

7. What was most helpful to you about the explanation of how we know we have the right Gospels in our Bibles, and how we can be confident the texts are accurate? Do you have any remaining questions on this subject? (pp. 32–35)

8. In what ways did chapter 1 help you think about the differences between the four Gospel accounts? What questions do you still have? (pp. 35–38)

9. After reading chapter 1, do you feel more or less convinced that Matthew, Mark, Luke and John are historically reliable accounts of Jesus's life? Why?

10. If the four Gospel accounts of Jesus's life *are* reliable testimony about him, what difference does that make to us today?

2

Jesus the Son

1. Which of these statements best represents your own thinking about Jesus at this point?

   a. Jesus never said he was God. The claims about him were exaggerated over time.

   _____

   b. Jesus did claim to be God, but he was deluded.

   _____

   c. Jesus claimed to be God because he truly is.

   _____

   d. I'm not sure. Still thinking all of this through.

   _____

2. Read Matthew 1:20–23. In what ways does Matthew point us to Jesus's divine identity? (pp. 42–45)

   _____

   _____

3. Read Mark 1:1–11. How does Mark communicate Jesus's divine identity? (pp. 45–46)

4. Read John 1:1–18. How does John's introduction add to what Mark and Matthew say about Jesus in the passages we've already looked at? (pp. 46–48)

5. Read Mark 2:1–12. How does Mark communicate Jesus's divine identity in this story? (pp. 48–49)

_____

_____

_____

_____

_____

6. Read John 14:1–9. In this passage, how does Jesus make an exclusive claim to be the one true God? (p. 56)

_____

_____

_____

_____

_____

7. Read John 20:24–29. How does Jesus react to Thomas's skepticism? (p. 57)

_____

_____

8. What difference does it make to us today if Jesus really is the one true God made flesh?

3

Jesus the King

1. What do you think of the idea that Jesus is God's long promised King? Does it feel like something you long for, or a threat to your freedom, or a ridiculous claim, or something else?

_____

_____

_____

_____

_____

2. The first sentence of Mark's Gospel reads, "The beginning of the gospel of Jesus Christ, the Son of God" (Mark 1:1). How would you put that sentence into your own words after reading pages 60–62?

_____

_____

3. Read Luke 4:16–22. What do we learn about Jesus's kingship from this passage? (pp. 63–64)

4. Did anything on pages 64–65 make you think differently about Jesus's impact on our understanding of ethics? If so, explain. Do you think that the arc of the moral universe *naturally* bends toward justice, or (like Dr. King) do you think that justice requires an ultimate judge?

5. Read Matthew 16:13–23. How do we see Peter's misunderstanding of Jesus's identity play out? (pp. 67–68)

6. Read Matthew 16:24–28. Jesus really raises the stakes here. He says that following him means dying but getting your real life back. He also says there's no point in gaining the whole world but losing your soul. What do you think of these claims? (p. 68)

7. Read John 4:7–30. Why is it striking that Jesus revealed his identity as "the Christ" to a Samaritan woman with a colorful history? How does the Samaritan woman's understanding of Jesus change? (pp. 70–71)

8. Read Matthew 26:57–68. How important is Jesus's identity as King in the process of him being condemned to death? (pp. 73–74)

9. Read Matthew 27:27–31. This is the only time in the Gospels that we see Jesus crowned. What does this troubling scene tell us about Jesus as King? (pp. 74–75)

_____

_____

_____

_____

_____

_____

10. Read Luke 23:32–43. Multiple people in this passage speak to Jesus as if he is a king, but only one of the criminals next to him actually believes that he is. How does Jesus react to this unlikely follower? What does it tell us about the kind of people Jesus welcomes into his kingdom? (p. 75)

_____

_____

_____

_____

_____

_____

_____

4

Jesus the Healer

1. Have you or someone close to you ever had a health crisis that really made you rethink what you believe? If so, explain.

_____

_____

_____

_____

_____

2. If Jesus is God's Son, do you think this means that praying to Jesus should always result in physical healing? Why or why not?

_____

_____

_____

3. Read Luke 5:27–32. What does Jesus's conversation with the Pharisees tell us about him, and what does it tell us about them? (pp. 78–79)

4. Read Mark 1:40–45. What is striking about Jesus's reaction to this man with leprosy? What's striking about the man's reaction to Jesus? (pp. 79–81)

5. Read Mark 5:21–43. According to the Gospels, Jesus healed hundreds, perhaps even thousands of people. Why do you think Mark picks out the healing of this bleeding woman and this dead twelve-year-old girl? (pp. 81–83)

6. A lot of people struggle with self-worth, and the remedy that tends to be offered to us is greater self-love, self-care, and self-belief. How does Jesus's interaction with the Roman centurion in Matthew 8:5–13 offer us a different answer to the challenge of self–worth? (pp. 83–84)

7. Read Matthew 15:21–28. How does this story build on the story of the Roman centurion's faith? (pp. 85–87)

8. What do you make of Jesus casting out demons or unclean spirits? Do you think it's naïve to believe in spiritual forces of evil, or do you think the existence of evil forces helps us to make sense of the world as we see it even today? (pp. 87–90)

9. Read John 9:1–40. How does this story help us understand the relationship between sin and physical sickness? (pp. 90–92)

10. Read Isaiah 53:4–5 and Matthew 8:14–17. How does Jesus's death on the cross help us to better understand his identity as the great healer? (pp. 92–93)

5

Jesus the Teacher

1. If you were to share this chapter with your primary friend group, work colleagues, or extended family, what might they find offensive in what it says about Jesus's teaching?

_____

_____

_____

_____

_____

_____

2. Read Matthew 7:3–5. How does this passage help us understand Jesus's use of hyperbole (extreme exaggeration) in his teaching? (pp. 96–98)

_____

_____

_____

3. Read Luke 10:25–37. Why does Jesus highlight the fact that the hero is a Samaritan? How does that help us better understand whom Jesus cares about? Why does it matter? (pp. 98–101)

4. Non-Christian historians like Tom Holland and Yuval Noah Harari agree that the idea of human equality and value came from Christianity. What difference do you think that makes today? Does it matter *why* people believe something as long as they believe it? (pp. 101–2)

5. Read Matthew 5:27–30 and Mark 7:21–23. How do these passages help us understand where sin comes from and how serious it is in Jesus's eyes? (pp. 102–4)

6. Read Luke 7:36–50. Why is this story surprising, in light of what Jesus taught about the seriousness of sin? (pp. 104–5)

7. Read Luke 16:19–31. How does this story make you feel and why? (pp. 105–8)

_____

_____

_____

_____

_____

8. How does Jesus's teaching on poverty "transform the status of the destitute"? (pp. 108–10)

_____

_____

_____

_____

_____

9. In Luke 15:11–32, Jesus tells a story about a son who squanders his inheritance and only comes back to his father when he's out of options. But still, his father is eager to welcome him back.

What does this reveal about God's heart toward those who turn to him? (pp. 111–12)

10. In what ways do the teachings of Jesus explored in this chapter affirm what you already believe, and in what ways do you feel offended or challenged? (p. 112)

6

Jesus the Lover

1. How would you define love?

_____

_____

_____

_____

_____

_____

2. Read Mark 2:18–20 and John 3:27–30. How does Jesus an-
nounce himself as the bridegroom? Who is the bride? (pp. 114–16)

_____

_____

_____

_____

3. Read Isaiah 54:5–8; Jeremiah 3:20; and Mark 2:18–20. How does God portray himself in the Old Testament passages? How does this help us understand the role Jesus is taking on? (p. 115)

4. How is God's love the original, and human romantic love (at its best) an imitation of that love? How does understanding this free us as we think about the place of romantic love in our own lives? (pp. 116–19)

5. Read Matthew 19:1–9. What do we learn about Jesus's view of marriage from this text? What do we learn from the reaction of his disciples? How do we see Jesus affirming both marriage and singleness in this passage? (pp. 119–25)

6. Why do you think marriage often gets promoted and singleness put down in Christian circles? How does Jesus's example as a single man and his teaching on singleness help us see things differently? (pp. 123–25)

7. Read John 15:12–13. How is Jesus's high view of friendship love displayed in these verses? How does this help us understand

a Christian view of same-sex love? What would it look like if we took these verses seriously in our own lives? (pp. 125–28)

_____

_____

_____

_____

_____

8. How does Jesus's high view of marriage and high view of friendship love counter the modern mantra that "love is love"? (pp. 126–27)

_____

_____

_____

_____

_____

9. What did you make of Rebecca's own story on pages 127–28?

_____

_____

10. Read John 18:15–18, 25–27. Then read John 21:7–17. How does Jesus's response to Peter's denial of him help us better understand Jesus's love? (pp. 128–29)

7

Jesus the Servant

1. Personal freedom is one of the highest values in our society. How does Jesus's presentation of himself as a servant, or even a slave, challenge the idea that unlimited freedom is the path to human happiness?

_____

_____

_____

_____

_____

_____

2. Read Exodus 20:1–3. In the Bible, we see that God frees his people from slavery but doesn't leave them as free agents. What

5

do these verses communicate about a right relationship with God? (pp. 132–34)

_____

_____

_____

_____

_____

3. Read Matthew 12:15–21. What are the characteristics of the Lord's servant according to these verses? How does Jesus, as we meet him in the Gospels, fit this description? (pp. 138–39)

_____

_____

_____

_____

_____

4. Read Mark 9:33–35 and 10:42–45. According to Jesus, what does greatness look like in God's kingdom? How does that go against our natural human instincts? (pp. 140–42)

_____

_____

5. In Mark 10:45, Jesus presents his death as a great exchange: he gives his life as a ransom for many. Do you find it hard to believe that Jesus gave his life for you specifically? If so, why? (pp. 142–44)

6. Read John 13:3–15. In the culture of that day, foot washing was the job of a servant or slave. Why does Jesus take that job himself on the night that he would be betrayed to his death? How could we follow Jesus's example of serving one another in the humblest ways possible today? (pp. 144–45)

7. How did Jesus's death on a Roman cross identify him with the slaves of that day? (pp. 146–47)

8. What difference does Jesus's identification with slaves and the oppressed make to how we think about Jesus today?

9. The history of White Christians' complicity in the enslaving of Black people is an important reason many people today dismiss Christianity. How does Jesus's identification with slaves help us to think about this?

10. If something is only worth as much as someone is willing to pay for it, and Jesus died for you, what does that mean about your worth to him? (pp. 147–48)

8

Jesus the Sacrifice

1. How is the idea of Jesus being the sacrifice for our sins both attractive and repulsive to people in our culture today? How does it strike you?

_____

_____

_____

_____

_____

_____

_____

2. Read Gen 22:1–14. How is Abraham almost sacrificing his son Isaac a preliminary sketch of Jesus's death on the cross for us?

How does this narrative help us better understand the heart of God the Father? (pp. 150–53)

_____

_____

_____

_____

_____

3. How was blood over the doorways a sign for the Israelites in Egypt? How does it point us toward Jesus's sacrifice? (pp. 153–54)

_____

_____

_____

_____

_____

4. Read John 1:29. What does John the Baptist mean when he calls Jesus "the Lamb of God"? (pp. 155–56)

_____

_____

5. Read John 2:18–22. What does Jesus mean when he identifies the temple with his body? (pp. 156–58)

_____

_____

_____

_____

_____

6. Read Psalm 23:1 and John 10:11–15. What do we learn from Jesus's description of himself as the good shepherd? How does this show that Jesus is not a passive victim when he dies on the cross? Why does this matter? (pp. 158–60)

_____

_____

_____

_____

7. Read Matthew 26:26–29. How does this passage help us to understand what Jesus's death means for his disciples? (pp. 160–61)

8. Read Isaiah 51:17, 21–23 and Matthew 26:36–46. How does the Old Testament metaphor of the cup of God's wrath help us understand what Jesus faced when he was crucified? (pp. 161–63)

9. What's the significance of Jesus voluntarily taking God's judgment for our sin upon himself? What does this tell us about the seriousness of our sin and the depth of Jesus's love for us? (pp. 163–66)

10. We saw in chapter 2 that the Gospels present Jesus as God the Son who became human, and how the Bible reveals God to us as Father, Son, and Spirit. What difference does this make as we think about Jesus dying on the cross and taking God's anger against our sin upon himself? (pp. 166–67)

9

Jesus the Lord

1. How did you feel about the introduction to this chapter, which described Nora Seed's disappointment with life and the chance she was given in *The Midnight Library* to try different versions of her life? Are there things in your past that you would go back and change if you could? Do you think it would make you feel more hopeful about your future if you could change your past? (pp. 169–70)

2. Read John 1:1–5. How does this passage present the Word—whom John identifies with Jesus—as the source of all life? (p. 171)

_____

_____

_____

_____

_____

_____

3. What do you picture when you think about eternal life? How is Jesus's promise of eternal life different from a promise of a life that just never ends? (pp. 171–74)

_____

_____

_____

_____

_____

_____

_____

4. Read John 11:17–27. What does Jesus claim about himself in this passage? How does his raising of Lazarus in John 11:43–44 support his claim to be the resurrection and the life? Why do you think Jesus focuses on resurrection, instead of just life without death? (pp. 174–77)

5. How compelling do you find the evidence for Jesus's resurrection? What evidence *would* you find persuasive? (pp. 177–84)

6. What difference does it make whether Jesus physically rose again or not? (pp. 184–85)

_____

_____

_____

_____

_____

7. Do you agree with this statement: "Love demands that we trade our independence for commitment to our loved ones' good"? (p. 186). If so, how have you seen this played out in your life?

_____

_____

_____

_____

_____

8. Read Matthew 28:16–20. Jesus claims to have been given all authority in both heaven and earth. What does he say his disciples should do in light of this? How do you feel about the idea that

Jesus is the rightful Lord of *all*—not just Lord of one ethnicity or country or racial group? How has this truth been abused at times in history, and what should it mean for us today? (pp. 186–87)

_____

_____

_____

_____

_____

_____

9. How do you feel about the claim that Jesus "conquered even death, so he's the rightful King of all who are alive. We have the opportunity today to welcome him . . . or else we can reject his rule—for now at least" (pp. 186–87). Why is there no middle ground when it comes to Jesus?

_____

_____

_____

_____

_____

_____

10. What do you think about Jesus as Lord? Have you trusted in him and asked him to be your Lord? Is there anything holding you back?

_____

_____

_____

_____

_____

_____

Also Available from Rebecca McLaughlin

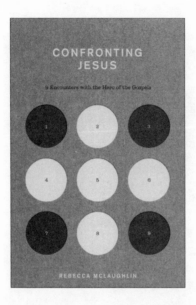

"Among the many books that have been written about Jesus, *Confronting Jesus* is one of the most carefully written, compelling, and convincing volumes I have seen. What makes it special is how thoughtful and accessible it is, not only to Christians but also to those who have questions or even doubts concerning faith. If you are looking for a resource to help you or a friend encounter and consider Jesus Christ as he really is, look no further. This is that resource."

SCOTT SAULS

Senior Pastor, Christ Presbyterian Church, Nashville, Tennessee; author, *A Gentle Answer* and *Beautiful People Don't Just Happen*

For more information, visit **crossway.org**.

A Video Companion to
Confronting Jesus

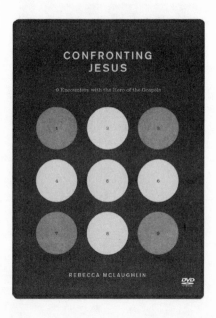

In the *Confronting Jesus Video Study*, McLaughlin hosts
one brief segment for each of the book's 9 chapters, as
well as an introduction and conclusion. An ideal resource
for small groups and personal study, these video lectures
can be used alongside the *Confronting Jesus* book and
Confronting Jesus Study Guide, inviting participants to
learn more about the person and work of Christ.

For more information, visit **crossway.org**.